The Surname Barr

Dr Susan Morris &
Wendy Bosberry-Scott

The question of surnames, their origins, distribution and history, lies at the heart of genealogy as well as being fascinating in its own right.

In the 1980s and 1990s, long before many genealogical sources were even indexed, let alone online, our Surname Report service provided expert assessments of the origins, history and distribution of selected British surnames, using the sources available at the time.

Now, with so many more sources available, we believe that these reports retain their value as studies of individual surnames, and so we are gradually making the Debrett Surname Archive available online and in print for the first time. Some modern indexes have been consulted to refresh and update the reports.

Debrett Ancestry Research Ltd, PO Box 379,
Winchester SO23 9YQ
Tel: 01962 841904
Email: info@debrettancestry.co.uk
Website: www.debrettancestry.co.uk

CONTENTS

Overview

The use of surnames in England began in the Norman period, when surnames were not necessarily hereditary but usually a form of description. Some described the individual's trade or profession; others were nicknames; some gave the father's Christian name; others gave the individual's place of residence or origin.

Different surnames might be used in different documents, or more than one surname given in one document. Early descriptions were fairly elaborate and by the thirteenth and fourteenth centuries these were simpler, but still variable, and indeed the instability of surnames continued until well into the seventeenth century.

Although some Normans would already have had hereditary surnames on their arrival in Britain, the passing on of a surname from generation to generation only became customary in Britain gradually during the course of the thirteenth and fourteenth centuries. At the end of this period most of the population apparently had surnames.

Variations in the spelling of a family's surname were common up to the early twentieth century. This is due in part to widespread illiteracy but also to the fact that society was simply less bureaucratic.

There are four main groups of surnames:

A - Local names, which describe a person by his place of residence or origin.

B - Occupational names, which describe a person by his trade or profession.

C - Surnames of relationship, which refer to the Christian name of the father or other important relative.

D - Nicknames or sobriquets, coined to describe a person in terms of his appearance or character.

The surname Barr has multiple possible origins, which fall with categories A, B and D.

P H Reaney's authoritative *Dictionary of English Surnames* suggests four origins of the name Barr and its variants:

(i) From place-names or topographical descriptions meaning hilltops, notably in Scotland, where the Gaelic word *barr,* meaning 'height or hill', has given rise to the place-name Barr in Ayrshire and Renfrewshire. Similarly, in Staffordshire, the area of Great Barr, which surrounds Barr Beacon, takes its name from the Welsh word *bar,* meaning 'top or summit'.

(ii) In Middle English and Old French, the word *barre* has the meaning 'barrier, gateway'; in Lincolnshire the word *bar* was used to denote an obstruction in a stream (P H Reaney, *Dictionary of English Surnames*). This might also give rise to a topographical surname (describing one who lives by such a barrier or gateway). The word Bar survives in the names of streets, gates and locations such as Temple Bar in London and Bootham Bar in York.

(iii) Reaney speculates that the name Barr could have derived in some instances as a nickname for a tall, thin ('bar-like' man) or as a metonymic for a maker of bars (Robert *Barremakere*, 1347, City of London).

(iv) Reaney also points to the French place-names Barre-de-Semilly in La Manche or Barre-en-Ouche in Eure. Richard *de Barra* in the Domesday Book is likely to have hailed from one of these locations.

To these we may add a fifth:

(v) The Irish surname scholar Edward MacLysaght notes that in Ireland that Barr may in a few cases derive from the anglicised form of the rare Gaelic name *O Baire*, 'descendant of Baire', which is more usually anglicised as Barry. However, most Irish examples are in Ulster and will be Scottish in origin.

We have included in this study the variants Barre, Barrs, Barra, Delebere, Le Barr, De la Barr and La Barre.

The earliest example of the name that has been found was Richard de Barra, from the Domesday Book, Somerset, 1086. Other medieval examples of the surname are as follows:

1155	Hugo Barre	Lincolnshire
12thc	Alexander Barre	York
1170	Edricius de la Barre	Staffordshire
1199	William de Barre	Staffordshire
c1216	Anger de la Barra	Clerkenwell, London
1210	Gilbert le Barrier	Sussex
1221	Gilbert Barre	Kent
1272	Maltida Barre	Buckinghamshire
1275	Peter de Bar	Lewes, Norfolk

1283	John ate Barre	Battle, Sussex
1296	Walter atte Barre	Merston, Sussex
1327	Walter le Barrer	Sussex
1340	Atkyn de Barr	Baillie of Ayr

From this list, Hugo and Alexander Barre might have been given the name Barre as a nickname, while the names of William de Barre, Peter de Bar and Atkyn de Barr are likely to derive from place-names. John ate Barre might have lived by the gateway into a town or castle, as might Gilbert le Barrier, who was probably one and the same as Gilbert Barre. It will be seen that this group (of surnames apparently associated with a barrier) is concentrated in Sussex.

In 1892 W J Hardy and W Page published *A Calendar to the Feet of Fines for London and Middlesex 1189-1485*, which provides a useful snapshot of surnames of the landowning classes of the day. (The fine was a means of conveying or settling freehold property.)

1193-4	William and Asceline de Barra, Cripplegate, London
1252-3	Vincent de la Barre, Westminster
1300-1	Hamo and Christiane de la Barre, St Clement Danes, London
1390-1	Sir Thomas Barre and Lady Elizabeth, Eggeswere, Middlesex

Interestingly, Hamo and Christiane de la Barre's transaction concerned 'premises in the park of St Clement Danes, without the Bar of the new Temple, London', suggesting that it might have been the Temple Bar (gateway to the City) that gave rise to their surname. Vincent de la Barre's deed related to premises in Westminster; that of William and Asceline de Barra, to three acres of land in the parish of St Giles without Cripplegate. Again, it is possible that these two examples derive from proximity to gates to the City of London. Sir Thomas Barre and his wife Elizabeth held property farther afield, in 'Eggeswere' (Edgware) and Little Stanmere (Stanmore) in Middlesex.

Distribution

The name Barr features in three of the current volumes of the *English Surnames Series* (which is very incomplete). The Oxford volume (by Richard McKinley) points out that William de la Barre who held lands in South Stoke in the late thirteenth century also appears in Hundred Rolls as William de la Borre.

Richard McKinley's Sussex volume cites examples from the twelfth century of the forms Barre, atte Barre and Barrer (the suffix 'er' was a common feature of topographical names in Sussex from the thirteenth century onwards). He notes in particular Walter atte Barre, a taxpayer at Merston, West Sussex, in 1296, who appears thirty years later as Walter le Barrer in 1327. Similarly, the name atte Barre occurs in East Sussex alongside the name Barrer. Another individual appears as both Barre and atte Barre, and his name is Latinised in documents as *Barrarius*. This flexibility of forms, with or without the suffix, continued in Sussex as late as the seventeenth century.

The Lancashire volume (also by Richard McKinley) contains a single reference to the surname and shows a similar phenomenon: William del Barre (1323) appears as William del Barres in 1323 and 1324. The addition of 's' or 'es' being added to the name in the medieval period was found in a number of other instances in Lancashire and probably has no grammatical meaning.

As noted above, one of P H Reaney's suggested groups of derivation for the surname points to Norman origin. A much older work, *The Norman People* (by 'Mr Avenel',

1874), drew names from the London Post Office Directory of the day and linked them with the names from medieval Norman documentation. For Barr he cites the names Gerard, Geoffry, Peter, Ralph and Tiger de Barra, of Normandy, which appear in Pipe Rolls. He also cites, from the *Monasticon Anglicanum* (1693: a history of medieval monastic foundations), the name Ralph Barre; and with no references he also mentions Geoffry, Peter and Richard Barre or De la Barre from the thirteenth century; and he states that 'The De la Barres or De la Baeres held Southam, Gloucester'.

H R Moulton's *Palaeography, Genealogy and Topography* (1930), an extensive sale catalogue of historical documents, provides a useful sample of early references to surnames. We found here two pre-1700 entries for the name Barr(e), one from Warwickshire (1693) and the other from Hertfordshire (1483):

> Indenture quadripartite between **John Barr**, yeoman, of Fletchamstead, Co. Warwick and Phillis his wife, Thomas Wedtnam, gent, of Graisley Castle, Co. Notts and Elizabeth his wife, Gilbert Cocks, gent, of Northampton upon Soare, Co. Notts and Mary his wife, John Baxter, gent, of Great Witley, Co. Worc and Ruth his wife, George Grant the elder, gent, of Solihull, Co. Warwick, and Robert his son of the same of the first, John Wright, baker of Solihull of the second, George Field, joiner of the same of the third and Joseph Cotterill, yeoman, of woodsfarm in Solihull of the fourth, part declaring the uses of a fine to be levied of messuages and land in Solihull aforeseaid. 27th March 1693 (signatures and marks of all parties - 13 seals - £2).

Ratification and confirmation by Thomas Bourghchier the younger, knight, Humphrey Talbot, knight, William Pykenham, Clerk, David ap Gwilym (Gli) ap Morgan esquire, John Tyrell of Beche, esquire, John Monteford, clerk, John Lyle esquire, Robert Scowell esquire, William Tey esquire, John Nalton and Thomas Ballys, clerk of the estate and interest of Walter Copynger in the office of parker of the parks of Knebworth called 'lez Grete parke and Litill parke' Co. Hertford. With pasture for one horse and three cows and 'wyndefeldewode' and brousyng within these parks and an annual rent of 6I. 20d. of the issues and profits of the manor of Knebbeworth (clause of entry and distraint if the rent be in arrears) granted to him by their [sic] writing date 3rd December, Richard III, by Thomas Bourghchier the elder, knight, and Isabel his wife, dau and heir of **John Barre, knight**, in name of seisin of the said rent Thomas and Isabel have delivered to the said Walter 12d. 5th December 1483 (ten seals - £10)'

In 1890 H B Guppy published his *Homes of Family Names in Great Britain*, still the only published work on surname distribution in Britain as a whole. His work was based on printed genealogies and a survey of county directories for the 1880s, in which he looked especially at the names of farmers, reasoning that they were among the most stable groups in society. Guppy found that the name Barr was one of the most frequently found surnames in Scotland at that time, with about twelve in ten thousand farmers holding the name, chiefly in the Glasgow area. (He restricted his study to names which appeared in a proportion of 7:10,000 or higher.) No other area showed a proportion of Barrs high enough to be included.

George F Black in *The Surnames of Scotland* (1946) also found that the surname Barr was most frequently found in the districts around Glasgow in the 1940s. Like Reaney, he states that Barr was derived from the place-name in Ayrshire or Renfrewshire, possibly from both, and provides some further early references of Bar, Barr and Barre:

1423	John Bar (or de Barre), burgess of Edinburgh
1551	Patrick Bar, witness in Glasgow
1554	William Barr, com burgess of Glasgow
1565	Robert Barre, barber, Knockoule
1612	Archibald Bar, burgess, Glasgow
1686	William Barr, Paisley

Black noted that all three variants of the name occurred in the Edinburgh marriage records and that the name Barr is sometimes difficult to distinguish from 'Barry' which also interchanged with Barre.

J J Kneen's *The Personal Names of the Isle of Man* (1937) found the surname on the island in the nineteenth century:

> **Barr**, local name from 'spots' or other circumscribed areas
> Manx parochial registers II 1811, 1829
> Manx parochial registers 9 1812
> Probably from residence near a barr or barrier by which certain streets and roads were closed at night.

Many of the sources available for charting surname distribution through the centuries are necessarily confined to the wealthier sectors of the population: in general, nobody wanted to know the names of the poor but the names of those with money or land were naturally of interest to the authorities. However, one source that covers the whole of the social spectrum is provided by English parish registers, the earliest of which began in 1538 following a mandate that all parish priests should keep a weekly record of all baptisms, marriages and burials that took place in their parish. A survey of a cross section of parish registers for the years 1601 and 1602 was carried out in 1910 by F K and S Hitching; incidences of a particular surname are noted by parish and county, although with no indication of numbers of references. In 1601, the name Barre was noted in St Dunstan's, Canterbury, Kent. In 1602, Barr was noted in Durham and Norfolk.

A useful guide to the distribution of surnames for the sixteenth, seventeenth and eighteenth centuries in England is provided by the indexes to wills proved at the Prerogative Court of (the Archbishop of) Canterbury, in London, which had superior jurisdiction over local ecclesiastical courts where wills were proved until 1858. The PCC thus provides a national index, although it is not a completely representative one, as testators whose wills were proved in the PCC were mostly among the wealthier members of society, and a disproportionate number of them were from London or Middlesex.

Very few entries appear in the PCC will indexes for the surname Barr (etc) in the fifteenth and sixteenth centuries and only two place-names are shown: London and Kent. All entries were for Barre, rather than Barr or another variant:

Fifteenth & Sixteenth Centuries
1439   John Barre of Markeley of Friars Minories, City
       of London
1485   Dame Jane Lady Barre, wife
1502   John Barre

1539   Richard Barre, clothier of Cranbrook, Kent

In the seventeenth century the PCC will indexes show a great many more entries for the surname, many with the suffix 's' which was a common addition at this period. All the De la Barr(e)s, apart from an isolated entry in Herefordshire, were from London. There was a single entry for Barra in Somerset (1650). Barr or Barre was found generally in the south-eastern counties of England, with something of a concentration in Berkshire. The PCC was the sole jurisdiction for testators who died abroad ('pts') or at sea, and so there are several mariners and expatriates in this list. The list also includes the will of a French expatriate, Vincent De La Barre (1617); the surname De la Barre survives today in France:

Seventeenth Century

1607   John Delabere, gent., Middle Temple, London
1612   John Barrs, citizen and clothworker, Hoxton, Middlesex
1612   Sibill Delabere, widow, Tibertown, County Hereford
1617   Vincent de La Barre, Hart Street, London - will in French
1626   Stephen Barre, husbandman, Seale, Kent
1642   Margaret Barre, widow of Lullingstone, Kent
1650   Morris Barra, husbandman of Portishead, Somerset
1658   Edmund Barr, yeoman, Bramber, Sussex
1658   John Barrs, mariner of the ship *Couvertine*, died in Jamaica in the service of this Commonwealth
1658   George Barr, labourer of Wilden, Bedfordshire
1657   Peter Barr, yeoman, Wantage, Berkshire (also known as Burr)
1658   George Barr, labourer, Wilden, Berkshire

1665 Richard de la Barre or Barr, distiller of Wapping (St Mary Whitechapel) Middlesex

1668 Mary de la Barre, widow, London

1677 John Barr, taylor, Coworth Old Windsor, Berkshire

1680 Peter Bar or Barr merchant of Oporto, Portugal

1681 Thomas Barr, the elder, Speen, Berkshire

1685 Peter Barr, Oporto, Kingdom of Portugal

1691 Abraham Barrs, cooper, London, (ship *Samuel and Mary*)

1692 Richard Barrs, mariner, HMS *Exeter*, (ship *Britannia*), of Whitechapel, Middlesex

1695 Richard Barr or Barre, distiller, London

1696 Mary De la Barre, wid., St Mary, Savoy Strand, Liberty of Westminster, alias Le Blanc/Blane

1698 William Barre, farmer, junr., Cippenham Green, Buckinghamshire

In the eighteenth century the majority of entries are from the south-east of England (mostly London and Middlesex) with single entries from Northamptonshire, Gloucestershire. There were several mariners, a French De la Barre from Paris and a La Barre (or La Baere or La Bare) from Jersey in the Channel Islands. The form Barr was now becoming dominant:

Eighteenth Century

1705 Judith Barr or Bar, widow of London

1708 Elizabeth de Bar de la Mothe of St Ann, Westminster, Middlesex

1709 Henry Barre, mariner being bound on a voyage to Borneo, of London

1709 Francis Berry or Barre, mariner now belonging to Her Majesty's ship *Assurance*

1712 Thomas Barrs, yeoman of Deptford, Surrey

1713 Harmon Barr alias Johnson, mariner bound to sea in the Ship *Hope*, Galley of Stepney, Middx

1716   John Barr, yeoman of Chipping Lambourn, Berkshire

1717   Richard Barr gentleman of St Martin in the Fields, Middlesex

1718   Elizabeth de la Barre, spinster of St Anne, Middlesex

1722   William Barr mariner of Bristol, Gloucestershire

1724   Anne Barrs, widow of St Olave Southwark, Surrey

1727   Julia Judith de la Barre alias de la Taille, widow of Paris, Kingdom of France

1736   William Barr of His Majesty's Ship *Buckingham*

1744   James Barr, mariner of St George, Middlesex

1746   Gratien de Bar de Manzac or Baron de Bar de Manzacs

1746   John Barr, outward bound in the Good Ship *Wager*

1750   James Barr, mariner late belonging to His Majesty's Ship *Dartmouth*

1760   Mary Barrs, widow of St Sepulchre, Middlesex

1760   Elizabeth Barr, Essex

1762   Alexander Barr, corporal of HM *Medway*, of Southampton

1762   Peter La Barre, Pts, alias La Baere, alias La Bare, mariner of St Helier, Jersey

1766   Elizabeth Barr, widow of Tottenham, Middlesex

1774   Tamar Barr, widow and farmer of St John, Hackney, Middlesex

1779   Richard Barr, miller of St Peter Brackley, Northampton

1781   John Barr, Pts, lately belonging to His Majesty's Ship *The Formidable*, now an invalid of Royal Hospital Plymouth, Devon

1782   Archibald Barr, Pts, serjeant of marines on board His Majesty's Ship *Warwick*

1787	Joseph Barr, merchant of St Andrew Holborn, Middlesex
1789	James Barr, bricklayer of St George Hanover Square, Middlesex
1790	John Barr, yeoman of Lambourne, Berkshire
1793	Pleasant Barr, widow of St Andrew Holborn, Middlesex
1795	John Barr, ticket porter of St Mary Whitechapel, Middlesex
1798	Eleanor Barr, widow of St George Hanover Square, Middlesex

In the nineteenth century the largest group, as we would expect, is from the metropolitan area, but the listing now shows a concentration of the name Barrs in the midland counties of Worcestershire, Staffordshire and Warwickshire. This may in part reflect a shift of wealth to the industrial heartland of England, but as we have seen, the name de (la) Barre, referring probably to the locality, was found in Staffordshire in medieval times.

It is interesting to see that the older form Barre now survives only in the upper echelons of society (1805, Mayfair) in which archaic forms are often preserved:

Nineteenth Century

1803	William Barr, wharfinger of St Olave Southwark, Surrey
1805	The Right Hon Isaac Barre of Mayfair, Middx
1808	Jane Barr, spinster of St Vedast Foster Lane, City of London
1809	James Smith Barr of St Martin in the Fields, Middx
1813	John Barr, tailor of Chipping Barnet, Hertfordshire
1813	Thomas Barr, bricklayer of St George Hanover Square, Middlesex

1814   Andrew Barr, china man of St James',
Middlesex

1814   Ruth Barrs, widow of St Marylebone,
Middlesex

1814   Mary Barr of St Marylebone, Middlesex

1814   Mary Barr, widow of North Shields,
Northumberland

1814   Martin Barr porcelain manufacturer of
Worcester

1815   William Barr, gentleman of Clifford's Inn,
London

1816   Richard Barr, tallow chandler of St
Barthlomew the Great, Middlesex

1818   William Barr of Hammersmith, Middlesex

1819   Patrick McClauchin or Mc Claughlin
otherwise Barr, formerly ostler now seaman on
the Hospital Ship *Wilhelmina* of Butcher Street,
Londonderry, County Londonderry

1820   John Barr of Wellington Place in the
Neighbourhood of Glasgow, Lanarkshire

1821   Martha Barr, single woman of Spilsby,
Lincolnshire

1821   William Barr, victualler of St Pancras,
Middlesex

1821   George Barrs, miller of Bramcote,
Warwickshire

1823   Reverend Thomas Barr of Coughton Court,
Warwickshire

1823   Sarah Tyzack Barr, spinster of Knightsbridge,
Middlesex

1823   Martha Barr, widow of Cloth Fair, city of
London

1823   Thomas Barr, bricklayer of Oxford,
Oxfordshire

1824   William Barr, assistant surgeon in the Royal
Navy

1825   George William Barr, gentleman of St Faith, Hampshire

1827   Joseph Barrs, gentleman of West Bromwich, Staffordshire

1827   Alexander Barr, surgeon and apothecary of Fletching, Sussex

1828   Jane Barr, spinster of Bartholomew Close, West Smithfield, Middlesex

1830   Angelar otherwise Angeler Barr, widow of St Faith, Hampshire

1830   Mary Barr [no other information shown in indexes]

1831   Mary Barrs, widow of Dudley, Worcestershire

1832   Walter Barrs, gentleman of Mountsorrel, Leicestershire

1834   Thomas Barr, butcher of Ratcliff Highway, St George, Middlesex

1835   John Barrs, maltster of West Bromwich, Staffordshire

1835   William Barrs, umbrella manufacturer of Birmingham, Warwickshire

1836   Thomas Barr, wharfinger of St Ann Limehouse, Middlesex

1836   Henrietta Barr, widow of Chipping Barnet, Hertfordshire

1838   William Barr, gentleman of Knaresborough, Yorkshire

1840   Thomas Barr, gentleman of Walthamstow, Essex

1840   Sarah Barrs, spinster of Birmingham, Warwickshire

1841   Charlotte Barr, spinster of St Marylebone, Middlesex

1841   Mary Selina Barr, spinster of Worksop, Nottinghamshire

1841   Reverend George Barrs, clerk, Master of Arts and Curate of Rowley Regis, Staffordshire

1841   Joze Barr or Joseph Barr or Jose Barr Crispin Deputy British Consul in the city of Faro and British Merchant of Faro, Kingdom of Portugal

1842   Jane Barrs, spinster of West Bromwich, Staffordshire

1843   John Barr, pensioner of Greenwich Hospital

1843   Thomas Barr, ironmonger of Lechlade, Gloucestershire

1844   Mary Barrs, widow of Rowley Regis, Staffordshire

1847   Elizabeth Barr, widow and shopkeeper of Lechlade, Gloucestershire

1847   James Callan Barr of Upper Kennington Lane, Surrey

1848   Martin Barr, captain of the Worcester Local Militia of Hallow, Worcestershire

1848   George Barr, captain of the Worcester local Militia of Hallow, Worcestershire

1848   Alexander Barr, assistant surgeon Royal Navy of Ayton, Berwickshire

1848   Charles Barr, banker of Leeds, Yorkshire

1849   George Thornton Barr, gentleman of Peckham, Surrey

1849   Richard Barr, gentleman of Alveston, Warwickshire

1852   Jeremiah Barr, gentleman of 3 St James Street, Upper Clapton, Middlesex

1854   William Frederick Barr, lieutenant in His Majesty's Navy of Bishops Waltham, Hampshire

1854   Martha Jane Barr, widow of Trafalgar Villa, Cold Harbour Road, Brixton, Surrey

1855   Edward Barrs, solicitor of Birmingham, Warwickshire

1856   Sarah Rayner Barr, widow of Clapham Rise, Surrey

1857   John Barr, gentleman of Greenwich, Kent

1857   James Barr of St Mary Islington, Middlesex

1857 Eliza Barr of New Windsor, Berkshire
1857 Joseph Barrs, maltster of West Bromwich,
      Staffordshire

For the nineteenth century, H B Guppy's survey has been mentioned above. Another important Victorian source for England is the *Return of Owners of Land* of 1873, sometimes known as the Modern Domesday Book. This source lists, county by county, every owner of an acre of land or more, with their residence (not necessarily the address of their property) and the acreage of their holding. This shows a thin scattering of entries throughout England (the metropolitan area was excluded from the survey), again with something of a concentration in the industrial midlands:

Return of Owners of Land

Berkshire	2	Barr
Buckinghamshire	1	Barrs
Lancashire	1	Barr
Leicestershire	3	Barrs
Lincolnshire	1	Barr
	1	Barrs
Nottingham	1	Barr
Oxfordshire	1	Barrs
Shropshire	1	Barr
Southampton	1	Barr
Staffordshire	2	Barr
Warwickshire	3	Barr
	4	Barrs
Worcestershire	5	Barrs
Worcestershire	1	Barr
Yorkshire, ER	2	Barr
Yorkshire, NR	1	Barr
	1	Barrs

Census indexes provide a broad picture of the spread of the name Barr and variants in Britain in the second half of the nineteenth century. Decennial census returns were instituted in England, Scotland and Wales in 1801, but personal returns survive from 1841 onwards. For Ireland in this period, only the 1901 census survives:

1851
Channel Islands: Barr (4)
England: Barr (1589); Barra (29); Barre (23); Barrs (282)
Isle of Man: Barr (11); Barrs (1)
Scotland: Barr (3399); Barra (8); Barrs (7)
Wales: Barr (1); Barra (3)

1861
Channel Islands: Barre (3)
England: Barr (1782); Barra (31); Barre (32);
        Barrs (363); La Barre (1)
Isle of Man: Barr (10)
Scotland: Barr (3657); Barra (7); Barrs (1)
Wales: Barr (6)

1871
Channel Islands: Barre (4)
England: Barr (2219); Barra (43); Barre (52);
        Barrs (415); La Barre (1)
Isle of Man: Barr (6)
Scotland: Barr (3979); Barra (13); Barre (4); Barrs (11)
Wales: Barr (11); Barre (5); Barrs (1)

1881
Channel Islands: Barr (1); Barre (6); La Barre (1)
England: Barr (2789); Barra (9); Barre (37); Barrs (467)
Isle of Man: Barr (8)
Scotland: Barr (4411); Barra (3); Barrs (4)
Wales: Barr (15); Barra (1); Barrs (1)

1891
Channel Islands: Barre (4)
England: Barr (3060); Barra (16); Barre (52); Barrs (511)
Isle of Man: Barr (7)
Scotland: Barr (4846); Barra (5); Barre (1); Barrs (1)
Wales: Barr (33); Barra (1); Barrs (5)

1901
Channel Islands: Barr (1); Barre (3)
England: Barr (3746); Barra (37); Barre (54);
            Barrs (651);
Isle of Man: Barr (7)
Scotland: Barr (5348); Barra (3); Barrs (3)
Wales: Barr (29); Barra (0); Barrs (7)
Ireland: Barr (1832); Barre (19); Barra (0); Barrs (4)

These figures support Guppy's conclusion that Scotland had the highest concentration of the surname Barr, but numbers were high too in Ireland. They need to be set against those for population growth in the nineteenth century: in England, for example, the population was just under 17 million in 1851, rising to over 30 million by 1901. Scotland saw an increase from just under 3 million in 1851 to around 4.5 million in 1901.

Census returns also provide a glimpse of how the name Barr developed in the United States, where the census was instituted in 1790. Prior to 1850 only the head of the household was named; from 1850 onwards, each member of the household was named. The 1890 census returns were destroyed by fire.

United States Federal Census Returns
1790
Barr (85); Barre (1); Barrs (2)

1800
Barr (128); Barre (2); Barrs (5)

1810
Barr (179); Barra (8); Barre (9); Barrs (10)

1820
Barr (340); Barra (7); Barre (8); Barrs (10)

1830
Barr (477); Barra (3); Barre (9); Barrs (16)

1840
Barr (696); Barra (4); Barre (19); Barrs (15)

1850
Barr (5481); Barra (62); Barre (209); Barrs (120);
La Barre (9)

1860
Barr (7170); Barra (58); Barre (209); Barrs (115)

1870
Barr (10,070); Barra (87); Barre (470); Barrs (140);
La Barre (6)

1880
Barr (12,004); Barra (62); Barre (553); Barrs (222);
De la Bar (7); La Barre (91)

1900
Barr (16,724); Barra (346); Barre (625); Barrs (393);
La Barre (32)

These figures show a massive influx of all forms, and particularly of the form Barr, in the second half of the nineteenth century, reflecting the growth of the population and the waves of immigration, particularly from Scotland and Ireland, at this time.

Scotland – Barr (5322); Barra (3); Barrs (3)
Wales – Barr (38); Barrs (4)

Distinguished bearers of the name

The *Dictionary of National Biography* (1st edition) for the British Isles includes three entries for the name Barre and one for Barr:

Isaac Barre (1726–1802), colonel and politician; graduated Trinity college, Dublin, 1745; served under Wolfe against Rochefort, 1757; MP for Chipping Wycombe, 1761-74 and Calne, 1774-90; adjutant-general and governor of Stirling, 1703-4; vice treasurer of Ireland and privy councillor; treasurer of navy, 1782.

Richard Barre (*fl* 1170–1202), ecclesiastic and judge; envoy to papal court at time of Becketts murder; keeper of the Great Seal, 1170; archdeacon of Ely, 1184?-96; justice of Kings Court, 1196.

William Vincent Barre (1760?–1869), author; born in Germany of Huguenot parents; served in the Russian navy; interpreter to Bonaparte against whom he wrote satiric verses and was compelled to fly to England in 1803; published 'History of French Consulate under Napoleon Buonaparte' who he scurrilously attacked.

Archibald Barr (1855–1931), inventor of range finders; graduated in engineering, Glasgow, 1876; professor and founder of engineering laboratories for York College, 1884-9 and Glasgow 1889-1913; With William Stroud founded the firm which designed naval range finders, height finders, fire control and other precision instruments.

There are nine coat(s) of arms listed in Burke's *General Armory* granted to families of the name Barr(e); there are also two granted to families named De la Barr(e).

Burke's Extinct and Dormant Baronetcies (2nd edition, 1841, page 617) lists Sir Robert Barr, Burgess of Glasgow, who was created a Baronet of Nova Scotia, 'but the date of the creation is not exactly known'. G E Cokayne in *The Complete Baronetage 1900-1909* adds that on 29th September 1628 for Robert Barr, burgess of Glasgow, was 'said to have been created a Baronet'; there are no further particulars and no lands were recorded in Nova Scotia. The title became dormant soon after 1628.

Printed Genealogies

The following references have been found to printed genealogies of families named Barr(e) and other forms:

Barr

Paterson, *History of Ayr and Wigton*, iii, 123

Paterson, *History of the County of Ayr*, I, 293

T H Mullin, *Families of Ballyrashane*, (County Antrim, 1969)

Barre

George Lipscombe M.D, *History of the County of Buckingham*, iv, 19, 345   (London 1847 -) 4 vols

George Baker, *History and Antiquities of the County of Northampton*, i, 19 (London 1822-1841) 2 vols, folio

C Platt, *Medieval Southampton, The Port and Trading Community AD 1000-1600*, 1973

Buntine-Barr

George Robertson, *Account of Families in Ayrshire*, I, 155

De la Barr

Miscellanea Genealogica et Heraldica, i, 283

Harleian Society, xv, 224

Summary

To conclude, the name Barr has multiple origins, with the strongest group being that based in Scotland and Ireland, deriving from Scottish place-names. In England a separate group, based on the English topographical description or place-name Barr, appears in Staffordshire in medieval times and possibly remained in the area until the modern period; there was certainly a strong concentration of the name in the midlands in the nineteenth century. Other families may have originally been named from proximity to a gate or barrier; others may have acquired the surname originally as a nickname. Finally, some instances may have been Norman in origin. The form Barrs grew in popularity from the seventeenth century, this being a common phenomenon with single-syllable surnames, but the most prevalent form in modern times is Barr, and in England the strongest concentration of Barr (etc) families has been found in the metropolitan area. Few examples have been found in the extreme south-west or north-west of England, or in Wales.

Sources Consulted

P H Reaney, *The Origins of English Surnames* (London: Routledge & Kegan Paul, 1967)

P H Reaney & R M Wilson, *A Dictionary of British Surnames* (Oxford: Oxford University Press, 3rd edition, 1995)

P H Reaney, *Dictionary of British Surnames* (London: Routledge & Kegan Paul, 2nd edition, 1976)

P Hanks & F Hodges, *A Dictionary of Surnames* (Oxford University Press, 1988)

M A Lower, *Patronymica Brittanica* (London, 1860)

C W Bardsley, *Dictionary of English and Welsh Surnames* (1901: reprinted, Baltimore: Genealogical Publishing Co, 1967)

C L'Estrange Ewen, *Guide to the Origin of British Surnames* (London: John Gifford, 1938)

H B Guppy, Homes of Family Names in Great Britain (London, 1890)

Ernest Weekley, *The Romance of Names* (London: John Murray, 2nd edition, 1917)

Ernest Weekley, *Surnames* (London: John Murray, 1917)

George F Black, *The Surnames of Scotland* (New York Public Library, 1946)

Edward McLysaght, *The Surnames of Ireland* (Dublin: Irish University Press, 1977)

T J & Prys Morgan, *Welsh Surnames* (Cardiff: University of Wales Press, 1985)

F K & S Hitching, *References to English Surnames in 1601* (Walton on Thames: Bernau, 1910)

F K & S Hitching, *References to English Surnames in 1602* (Walton on Thames: Bernau, 1911)

Debrett's People of Today (Debrett's Peerage Limited: London, 1996)

The Oxford Dictionary of National Biography (online, 2004–2014)

The Concise Dictionary of National Biography, Part II, 1901–1950, (Oxford, 1961)

Burke's Family Index (London: Burke's Peerage Limited, 1976)

Burke's Extinct and Dormant Baronetcies (London: 2nd edition, 1841)

H R Moulton, *Palaeography, Genealogy & Topography* (Sale Catalogue, 1930)

Index to Prerogative Court of Canterbury Wills (The National Archives: online)

G W Marshall, *The Genealogist's Guide* (1903; reprinted, Baltimore: GPC 1973)

J B Whitmore, *A Genealogical Guide* (London, 1953)

Charles Bridge, *An Index to Pedigrees* (London, 1867)

Geoffrey B Barrow, *The Genealogist's Guide* (London: Research Publishing Co, 1977)

Sir Bernard Burke, *The General Armory* (London, 1884)

C R Humphrey-Smith, editor, *Burke's General Armory Volume II,* (Tabard Press, 1973)

The Return of Owners of Land (1873)

Eilert Ekwall, *The Concise Oxford Dictionary of English Place-Names* (Oxford: Clarendon Press, 4th edition, 1960)

E G Withycombe, *The Oxford Dictionary of English Christian Names* (Oxford: Clarendon Press, 2nd edition, 1950)

W J Hardy & W Page, A Calendar to the Feet of Fines for London and Middlesex: Vol 1 Richard I – Richard III (1189–1485) (London, 1892)

Richard McKinley, *The Surnames of Oxfordshire* (English Surnames Series III: Leopard's Head Press, 1977)

Richard McKinley, *The Surnames of Sussex* (English Surnames Series V: Leopard's Head Press, 1988)

Richard McKinley, *The Surnames of Lancashire* (English Surnames Series IV: Leopard's Head Press, 1981)

Richard McKinley, *Norfolk and Suffolk Surnames in the Middle Ages* (English Surnames Series II: Phillimore, 1975)

George Redmonds, *Yorkshire West Riding* (English Surnames Series I: Phillimore, 1973)

The Norman People (London, 1874)

Debrett's Heraldry (London, 1933)

J P Brooke-Little, revised, *Boutell's Heraldry* (Frederick Warne: London, 1970)

Indexes to 1841–1911 Census Returns of England and Wales (The National Archives/*Ancestry.com*)

ScotlandsPeople: Indexes to Old Parish Registers, Testaments, Statutory Registers

Census Indexes 1851–1901 (*Ancestry.co.uk, ScotlandsPeople,* National Archives of Ireland)

www.ingramcontent.com/pod-product-compliance
Lightning Source LLC
Chambersburg PA
CBHW061931280526
45787CB00004B/1571